The Star Wizard's Legacy

BOOKS BY MORTON MARCUS

Origins (Kayak, 1969)

Where The Oceans Cover Us
(Capra, 1972)

The Santa Cruz Mountain Poems
(Capra, 1972; Capitola Book Company, 1992)

The Armies Encamped In The Fields Beyond The Unfinished Avenues: Prose Poems
(Jazz Press, 1977)

Big Winds, Glass Mornings, Shadows Cast By Stars: Poems, 1972-1980
(Jazz Press, 1980)

The Brezhnev Memo
(Dell/Delacorte, 1981) Novel

Pages From A Scrapbook Of Immigrants
(Coffee House, 1988)

When People Could Fly: Prose Poems
(Hanging Loose, 1997)

Moments Without Names: New & Selected Prose Poems
(White Pine Press, 2002)

Shouting Down The Silence: Verse Poems 1988-2001
(Creative Arts, 2002)

Pursuing The Dream Bone: New Prose Poems
(Quale Press, 2007)

Striking Through The Masks: A Literary Memoir
(Capitola Book Company, 2008)

— EDITOR —

In A Dybbuk's Raincoat: The Collected Poems of Bert Meyers,
with Daniel Meyers (University of New Mexico Press, 2007)

THE STAR WIZARD'S LEGACY

Six Poetic Sequences

VASKO POPA

Translated By
MORTON MARCUS

TERRA INCOGNITA SERIES, VOLUME 11

WHITE PINE PRESS / BUFFALO, NEW YORK

Acknowledgments: "Remembering Vasko Popa" originally appeared in a slightly different form entitled "Vasko Popa" in *Striking Through The Masks: A Literary Memoir* by Morton Marcus, published by Capitola Book Company, 2008.

A different version of the translation of "Give Me Back My Little Rags," by Morton Marcus and Charles Simic, originally appeared in *Ploughshares*.

Publication of this book was made possible, in part, with public funds from the New York State Council on the Arts, a State Agency.

Cover art and drawings thoughout the book are by Fernando Mercado. Copyright ©2010 by Fernando Mercado. Used by generous permission of the artist.

Photographs are by Joel Leivick. Copyright ©2010 by Joel Leivick. Used by generous permission of the photographer.

First Edition.

ISBN: 978-1-935210-11-5

Printed and bound in the United States of America.

Library of Congress Control Number: 2009932979

WHITE PINE PRESS
P.O. Box 236
BUFFALO, NEW YORK 14201

www.whitepine.org

CONTENTS

*This book is dedicated to all translators,
who labor to bring the words and visions
of other cultures into their own language.*

INTRODUCTION

Vasko Popa in California, 1970

The following poems were translated by Vasko Popa and me in the spring of 1970 when Popa was visiting the United States as part of an international poetry forum in Washington DC. After the forum, Popa traveled to the West Coast where I was his host for the State Department, and we prepared for his readings at Cabrillo College, where I taught, and at The University of California at Berkeley, where future Nobel Laureate Czeslaw Milosz sponsored his appearance. For five days Popa and I sat together polishing the poems, working from recent translations by Charlie Simic and published translations by Popa's official translator, Anne Pennington. With us was Popa's State Department translator, a Slovenian, who had accompanied Popa on his several readings across the country. Popa spoke almost no English and the process was difficult but rewarding — and a lot of fun for both of us. In the end, Popa proclaimed that these translations best captured the spirit of his poems in English and hoped that I could get them to Simic before he published his versions. Unfortunately, it was too late for that.

Popa also felt loyalty to Pennington, his British translator, and he made it clear he didn't want me to publish these translations on my own. For the past thirty-nine years I have honored that request. Meanwhile, both Popa and Pennington have long since shaken off their mortal coils; Charlie's translations went out of print in the early 1980s, but were reisued in 1987; and the Pennington translation, incorporated into an expanded collected poems, was published in Britain in 1996, fifteen years after her death. Those translations have held sway for more than forty years, and I think it high time to bring another version of Vasko's singularly original work to the American reading public, if not the British.

These are the sequences we read from at Cabrillo and Berkeley, all except "Give Me Back My Little Rags," which

Charlie Simic and I worked on together and Charlie published in a different form years later in *Ploughshares* and I publish here in our original versions. Except for minor alterations to smooth the English phrasing, I have left the poems as they were translated during those fateful five days, which I have always remembered with great joy. I hope some of that joy will be experienced by the reader who has not encountered Vasko Popa's extraordinary poetry until now.

— Morton Marcus
Santa Cruz, California
2009

TRANSLATOR'S NOTE: "The Little Box" was not published in a book in Popa's lifetime. It was projected in a volume to be called *Iron Garden*. That doesn't mean that parts of the poem weren't published. Popa would work on poems over years and publish segments of them, and "The Little Box" was one of those. I worked on the sections here with Vasko. Years later, he added three more sections: "The Admirers of The Little Box," "The Owners of The Little Box," and "The Benefactors of the Little Box." To go along with the personal nature of the translations in this volume, I thought fit not to include those sections. Charlie Simic and I worked together on "Give Me Back My Little Rags."

BONE TO BONE

I. In The Beginning

Now it's easy
We're saved from flesh

What do we do now
Say something

Would you like to be
Lightning's backbone

Say some more

What shall I say
Hurricane's hipbone

Say something else

That's all I know
Heaven's ribs

We're nobody's bones
Say something else

II *After The Beginning*

What shall we do now

That's a good question
Now we'll have marrow for supper

We had marrow for lunch
There's a hollow feeling inside me

Then we'll make music
We like music

What will we do if the dogs come
They like bones

We'll stick in their throats
And have some fun

III. In The Sun

How wonderful sunbathing naked
I never cared much for flesh

Me neither those shreds didn't fool me
I'm crazy about you so naked

Don't let the sun caress you
Let's caress each other

But please not here not in the sun
Here all can see us dear bony

IV. Underground

Muscle of darkness muscle of flesh
They come to the same thing

Well what shall we do now

We'll invite all the bones from all times
We'll bake in the sun

What shall we do then

Then we'll grow pure
Go on growing just as we please

What shall we do after that

Nothing we'll wander here and there
We'll be eternal bone beings

Well then let's just wait
For the earth to yawn

V. In The Moonlight

What's that
It's as if some snowy flesh
Were clinging to me

I don't know what it is
It's as if marrow was coursing through me
Cold marrow

I don't know either
It's as if everything were beginning again
With a more horrible beginning

Let me ask you something
Can you bark

VI. Before The End

Where shall we go now

Where should we go nowhere
Where else would two bones go

What'll we do there

There waiting for us a long time
There eagerly expecting us
Are no one and his wife nothing

What use are we to them

They are old they are without bones
We'll be like daughters to them

VII. The End

I am a bone you are a bone
Why have you swallowed me
I can't see myself anymore

What's wrong with you
It's you who've swallowed me
I can't see myself either

Where am I now

Now no one knows any more
Who is who nor who is where
Everything is an ugly dream of dust

Can you hear me

I can hear both you and me
There's the spur of a rooster's leg
Crowing out of us

(1956)

THE LITTLE BOX

I. The Little Box

The little box grows her first teeth
And her little length
Her little width her little emptiness
She has everything else

The little box keeps growing
The cupboard is inside her
That she was inside before

And she grows big big bigger
Now the room is inside her
And the house and the city and the landscape
And the world she was inside before

The little box remembers her childhood
And in a great big wish
She becomes a little box again

Now inside the little box
is the whole world in miniature
It can easily be put in a pocket
Easily stolen easily lost

Take care of the little box

II. The Craftsmen of the Little Box

Don't open the little box
The cap of heaven will fall out

Whatever you do don't close her
She'll slice the trouser leg of eternity

Don't drop her on the ground
The sun's eggs will smash inside her

Don't throw her in the air
The earth's bones will shatter inside her

Don't hold her in your hands
The stars' dough will sour inside her

What are you doing for heaven's sake
Don't let her out of your sight

III. The Tenants of the Little Box

If you toss a stone
Into the little box
You'll take out a bird

If you toss in your shadow
You'll take out the shirt of happiness

If you toss in your father's root
You'll take out the axle of the universe

The little box works for you

If you toss a mouse
Into the little box
You'll take out a quaking hill

If you toss in your mother's skull
You'll take out the chalice of eternal life

If you toss in your head
You'll take out two

The little box works for you

IV. The Enemies of the Little Box

Don't bow down to the little box
Which seemingly contains everything
Your star and every other star

Empty yourself
In her emptiness

Take all the nails out of her
And give them to her owners
So they can eat them

Make a hole in her middle
And stick in your clapper

Stuff her with blueprints
And the skin of her builders
And trample her with both feet

Tie her to the cat's tail
And chase the cat

Don't bow down to the little box
If you do
You'll never get up again

V. The Victims of the Little Box

You should have nothing to do
with the little box
even in your dreams

If you see her full of stars
You'll wake up
Without heart or soul in your chest

If you slide your tongue
Into her keyhole
You'll wake up with a hole in your forehead

If you rip her into pieces
with your teeth
You'll get up with a square head

If you ever see her empty
You'll wake up
With a belly full of mice and nails

If you ever have business in a dream
With the little box
You better not wake up

VI. The Judges of the Little Box

Why do you gape at the little box
Which in her emptiness
Holds the entire world

If the little box holds
The world in her emptiness
Then the anti-world
Holds the little box in its anti-hand

Who will bite off the anti-world's anti-hand
With its
Five hundred anti-fingers

Do you really think
You can bite it off
With your thirty-two teeth

Or are you waiting
For the little box
To leap into your mouth by itself

Is this why you are gaping

VII. The Prisoners of the Little Box

Open little box

We kiss your bottom your lid
Your keyhole and key

The entire world lies squashed inside you
It looks like anything
but itself

Not even mother serenity
would recognize it any more

Rust will eat your key
Our world and us inside you
And in the end you too

We kiss your four sides
And four corners
And twenty-four nails
And anything else that's yours

Open little box

VIII. Last News of the Little Box

The little box which contains the world
Fell in love with herself
And gave birth
To another little box inside her

The little box of the little box
Also fell in love with herself
And gave birth
To yet another little box inside her

And so it goes forever

Now the world in the first little box
Should be somewhere in the last box
born of all the little boxes

But none of the little boxes
Inside the little box in love with herself
Is the last one

Let's see you find the world now

THE WHITE PEBBLE

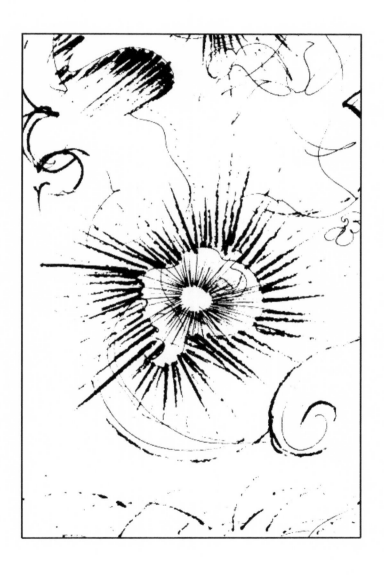

I. The White Pebble

Without a head without limbs
It emerges
From the excited pulse of chance
It moves
With the bold steps of time
It holds everything
In its passionate inner embrace

A white smooth virgin body
It smiles with the eyebrow of the moon

II. The Heart of the White Pebble

They played with the pebble
The pebble like any pebble
Played with them as though it had no heart

They got mad at the pebble
Smshed it in the grass
Startled they saw its heart

They opened the pebble's heart
In the heart a snake
A sleeping spool without dreams

They woke the snake
The snake leaped up
They ran far away

They watched from a distance
The snake coiled around the horizon
And ate it like an egg

They came back to the place of the game
No snake no grass no pieces of pebble
No trace of anything far and wide

They exchanged looks and grinned
They winked at each other

III. The Dream of the White Pebble

A hand rose out of the earth
Threw the pebble in the air

Where is the pebble
It didn't return to earth
It didn't reach heaven

What happened to the pebble
Did the heights swallow it
Did it turn into a bird

Here is the pebble
It remained stubbornly inside itself
Neither on earth nor in heaven

It obeys only itself
A world among other worlds

IV. The White Pebble's Love

It fell for beautiful
Round blue-eyed
Frivolous eternity

It has changed into
The white of her eye

Only she understands it
Only her embrace
Has the shape of its desire
Dumb and endless

It has captured
All her shadows in itself

Blindly in love
It sees no other beauty
Except the one it loves
Who will cost it
Its life

V. The Adventure of the White Pebble

Fed up with the circle
The perfect circle around it
It stopped short

Its burden is heavy
The burden inside it
It drops it

The stone is hard
The stone it was made of
It left behind

It was cramped where it lived
In its own body
It stepped out of it

It has hidden from itself
Hidden in its own shadow

VI. The Secret of the White Pebble

It has filled itself with itself
Gorged itself on its hard flesh
Is it sick

Ask it don't be afraid
It doesn't beg for bread

It is petrified in an ecstatic cramp
Is it pregnant
Will it give birth to a stone
Or to a beast or to a lightning streak

Ask it as much as you like
Don't expect an answer

Expect only a lump on the head
Or a second nose a third eye
Or who knows what

VII. Two White Pebbles

They stare at each other dully
Two pebbles looking at one another

Two candies yesterday
On the tongue of eternity
Two stone tears today
On the eyelid of the unknown

Two flies of sand tomorrow
In the ears of deafness
Two happy dimples tomorrow
In the cheeks of daylight

Two victims of a little joke
Dumb joke without a joker

They stare at each other dully
With their cold asses they stare
They speak out of their bellies
They speak hot air

(1951-1954)

GAMES

I. Before Playing

Shut an eye
Look into every corner of yourself
To see there are no spikes no robbers
No cuckoo's eggs

Now shut the other eye
Crouch and jump
jump high high high
To the top of yourself

From there let your weight pull you down
You'll fall for days far far far
To the bottom of your abyss

If you don't get smashed to smithereens
If you remain in one piece and get up in one piece
You can play

II. Floornail

One is the nail another is pliers
The rest are workmen

The pliers grab the nail by the head
They grab it with their teeth their arms
And tug tug it
Until they tug it out of the floor
Usually they just wrench off its head
It's hard pulling a nail out of the floor

Then workmen say
These pliers are no good
They smash their jaws break their arms
And throw them out the window

Then someone else is a floornail
Another is pliers
The rest are workmen

III. Hide and Seek

Somebody hides from somebody else
He hides under his tongue
The other looks for him underground

He hides in his forehead
The other looks for him in heaven

He hides in his forgetfulness
The other looks for him in the grass

Looks for him and looks for him
Looks for him in all sorts of places
And in looking for him loses himself

IV. Seducer

One caresses the leg of a chair
Until the chair moves
And motions him coyly with her leg

Another kisses a keyhole
Keeps kissing it and how
Until the keyhole returns the kiss

A third one stands to the side
Watches the other two
And shakes and shakes his head

Until his head drops off

V. Wedding

Each takes off his skin
Each exposes his constellation
Which has never seen the night

Each fills his skin with rocks
Starts dancing with it
By the light of his own stars

The one who doesn't stop till dawn
The one who doesn't blink or fall
He's the one who earns his skin

(This game is rarely played)

VI. The Rose Thieves

Someone is a rosebush
Several are the wind's daughters
Others the rose thieves

The rose thieves sneak up on the rosebush
One of them steals a rose
Hides it in his heart

The wind's daughters appear
See the plundered rosebush
And chase the rose thieves

They open the thieves' chests one by one
In some they find hearts
In others so help me nothing

They continue opening the thieves' chests
Until they discover the right heart
And in that heart the stolen rose

VII. Between Games

Nobody's resting

One is re-locating his eyes all the time
He places them on his back
And without wanting to walks backwards
He places them on the soles of his feet
And without wanting to returns walking on his head

Another has turned into an ear
And heard all that cannot be heard
But he gets sick and tired of it
And longs to become himself again
But without eyes he doesn't see how

Another has uncovered all his faces
And throws each in turn over the roof
The last one he throws under his feet
And buries his head in his hands

Another has stretched his view of things
Stretched it from thumb to thumb
And walks back and forth along its length
Slowly at first then fast
Then faster and faster

Another plays with his head
Tosses it in the air
And catches it on his index finger
Or doesn't catch it at all

Nobody's resting

VIII. Chase

Those on one side bite off the others'
Arm or leg or anything

Hold it in their teeth
Run as fast as they can
Bury it in the ground

The others chase all around
Sniffing seeking sniffing seeking
Dig up all the ground

If they are lucky enough to find their arm
Or leg or anything
It's their turn to bite

The game goes at a brisk pace

While there are arms
While there are legs
While there is anything

IX. Seed

Someone plants someone else
Plants him in his own head
Stamps the soil hard

Waits for the seed to sprout

The seed hollows out his head
Turns it into a mousehole
The mice eat the seed

They drop dead on the spot

The wind sets up house in the empty head
And gives birth to shifting breezes

X. Leap Frog

Each is a stone on the other's heart
Two stones like houses
Neither can budge under his stone

And both strain
To lift a finger
To click their tongue
To move their ears
At least to blink

Neither can budge under his stone

And both strain and strain
Exhaust themselves and fall asleep
And only in sleep can their hair stand up

(This game lasts a long time)

XI. Hunter

Somebody goes in without knocking
Goes into another's ear
And leaves through the other one

Goes in with a match step
With the step of a lit match
Roams around inside the head

He's made it

Somebody comes in without knocking
Goes into another's ear
And does not leave through the other one

He's cooked

XII. Ashes

Some are nights others stars

Each night sets fire to its star
And dances a black dance around it
Until the star burns out

Then the nights split up
Some become stars
The others remain nights

Again each night sets fire to its star
And dances a black dance around it
Until the star burns out

The last night becomes both star and night
It sets fire to itself
Dances the black dance around itself

XIII. After the Game

Finally the hands clutch the belly
So the belly won't burst from laughing
But there is no belly there

One hand can hardly rise
To wipe the cold sweat from the forehead
There is no forehead either

The other hand grabs for the heart
So the heart won't jump out of the chest
There is no heart either

Both hands fall
They fall slackly into the lap
There is no lap either

On one hand now the rain is falling
Out of the other grass grows
What more can I say

(1954)

Give Me Back
My Little Rags

Just fall into my mind
My thoughts will claw your cheek

Just crawl in front of me
My eyes will growl at you

Just open your big mouth
My silence will crack your jaws

Just remind me of what you are
My memory will dig a hole beneath your feet

That's how things stand between us

I.

Give me back my little rags

My rags of pure dream
Of silk smiles of striped warnings
Of my lacy sinews

My rags of polka-dot hope
Of filigreed lust of calico glances
Of the skin off my face

Give me back my little rags
I'm asking you nicely

II.

Listen monster
Off with your white kerchief
We know each other

Together from childhood
Lapping at the same bowl

Sleeping in the same bed
Evil-eyed knife

Walking this strange world
Snake in the shirt

Listen hypocrite
Off with your white kerchief
Why lie to each other

III.

I won't carry you on my back
I won't ferry you around any more

Not even if I were shod in gold
And harnessed to three wheels
On the cart of the wind
Not even if I were bridled to a rainbow

Don't try to bribe me

I won't carry you even with my feet in my pocket
Even threaded through a needle tied into a knot
Or carved into a simple stick

Don't try to scare me

I won't even roasted or overdone
Not raw not salted
Not even in a dream

Don't go on kidding yourself
It doesn't work now I won't

IV.

Get out of my walled-in infinity
Out of the dancing ring of stars around my heart
Out of my morsel of sunlight

Get out of my giggling sea of blood
Out of my flow my ebb
Out of my marooned silence

Get out I said out

Get out of my living void
Out of the bare ancestral-tree within me

Get out how long do I have to shout

Get out of my head bursting into pieces
Get out just get out

V.

You get kewpie doll notions
I bathe them in my blood
Dress them in my rags of skin

I make swings of my hair for them
Toy carts from my vertebrae
Kites from my eyebrows

I make them butterflies from my smiles
From my teeth wild beasts
To hunt to kill time

What kind of game is this anyway

VI.

Screw your root blood and crown
And everything else in your life

Screw every dried-up image in your brain
Every shifty eye burning its ember on your fingertip
Screw every step you take

Sink into three kettles of sour water
Into three stoves of prophetic fire
Into three pits without names or milk

An icy breath against your throat
Against the stone beneath your left tit
Against the bird-shaped razor in that stone

Swoop blackest of blackbirds to the lair of nothing
To the hungry scissors of all beginnings
To that womb of heaven I know so well

Screw your seed sap and glitter
Your darkness and the period at my life's end
And everything else in the world too

VII.

What happened to my little rags
Why won't you give them back why

I'll scorch off your eyebrows
You won't be invisible forever

I'll mix up day and night inside your skull
You'll bang your forehead against my back door

I'll pare away your screeching fingernails
You won't chalk hopscotch through my brain anymore

I'll suck the fog out of your bones
Slurp the hemlock off your tongue

You'll see what I can do

VIII.

So you want us to love each other

You can knead me from my ashes
From the shards of my bellylaughs
From what's left of my boredom

You can do that doll-face

You can grab me by the braid of loss
Hug my night in its empty shirt
Kiss my echo again and again

You don't even know what love is

IX.

Run monster

Our footprints bite one another
Bite one another in the dust behind us
We're not meant for each other

I see through your coldness
Walk through you from end to end
This isn't much of a game

How come we tied our rags together

Hand them over what do you want with them
It's foolish for them to fade on your shoulders
Hand them over and scram into your nowhere

Run monster from another monster

Where are your eyes
There's a monster here too

X.

May your tongue be black your noon your hope
Everything black only my chill white
My wolf at your throat

May the storm be your bed
Fear of me your pillow
Wide your sleepless field

May fire be your food wax your teeth
Come on glutton chew
Chew all you want

Silent your wind your water your flowers
Everything silent only my grinding teeth loud
My hawk at your throat

Leave let your mother live without your horror.

XI.

I rubbed your face off my face
Ripped your shadow off my shadow

Levelled the hills with you
Raised your plains into hills

Made your seasons quarrel
Kicked the earth's corners away from you

Closed my living path around you
My overgrown my impossible path

Now just try to find me

XII.

That's enough of your tender herbs
Of your sweet trifles
I don't want to hear to know
Enough enough of everything

I'll say my final enough
Stuff my mouth with dirt
Grind my teeth

I'll say goodbye skull-chewer
Goodbye once and for all

I'll stand as I am now
Without root branch or crown
I'll lean on myself
On my own welts

I'll be the stake slammed into you
Into you party-pooper
You bumble-brain
That's all I can be

Don't ever come back

XIII.

Don't mess with me

You hid a knife beneath your kerchief
Stepped over the boundary tripped me up
You spoiled the game

You wanted heaven to turn over
The sun to break my head
My little rags to be scattered

Monster never fool with another monster

Give me back my little rags
And I'll give you back yours

(1956)

(Translated by Charles Simic & Morton Marcus)

THE YAWN OF YAWNS

I. The Star Wizard's Legacy

He left behind his words
Lovelier than the world
No one dares look at them

They wait at the corners of time
Greater than people
Who can pronounce them

They lie on the dumb earth
Heavier than life's bones
Death could not carry them away
As his dowry

No one can lift them
No one can strike them down

Falling stars hide their heads
In the shadows of his words

II. Forgetful Number

Once upon a time there was a number
Pure and round like the sun
But it was lonely very lonely

It started to calculate itself

It divided multiplied itself
Subtracted and added itself
But it always remained alone

It stopped calculating
And shut itself up
In its round sunlit purity

The glowing tracks of its calculations
remained outside

They began to chase each other in the dark
To divide themselves while multiplying
To subtract themselves while adding

That's how things go in the dark

And there was no one to ask it
To stop its tracks
And erase them

III. The Arrogant Mistake

Once upon a time there was a mistake
So absurd so small
That no one would have noticed it

But it couldn't stand
To see or hear itself

It thought up many things
Just to prove
That it didn't really exist

It thought up space
In which to exhibit the proof
Time to guard the proof
And the world to see the proof

The things it thought up
Were neither as absurd nor as small
As it was
But they were of course wrong

What else could they have been

IV. The Philosophic Triangle

Once upon a time there was a triangle
It had three sides
The fourth it hid
In its blazing center

By day it would climb its three summits
And admire its center
At night it would rest
In one of its three angles

Each dawn it would watch its three sides
Turn into three incandescent wheels
That vanished into the blue of no return

Then it would take out its fourth side
Kiss it break it three times
And hide it where it had before

And again it had only three sides

And again each day it would climb
To its three summits
And admire its center
And at night rest
In one of its three angles

V. The Stone Echoes

Once upon a time there was an infinity of echoes
They were slaves of one voice
Built it arcades

The arcades tumbled down
They'd built them crooked
The dust covered them

They quit the dangerous job
Got so hungry they turned to stone

Now stone they flew off
To find and rip to pieces the lips
From which the voice spoke

No one knows how long they flew
The blind fools didn't see
That they flew along the very edge of the lips
They were looking for

VI. The Story About a Story

Once upon a time there was a story

It ended
Before it began
And began
After it ended

Its heroes entered it
After their death
And left it
Before they were born

Its heroes talked
About an earth and a heaven
They talked about many things

The only thing they didn't talk about
Was what they didn't know
That they are heroes in a story

In a story that ends
Before it begins
And begins
After it ends

VII. The Yawn of Yawns

Once upon a time there was a yawn
Not under the palate not under the hat
Not in the mouth not in anything

It was bigger than everything
Bigger than its own bigness

From time to time
Its dull night its hopeless night
Would glitter desperately here and there
You could imagine they were stars

Once upon a time there was a yawn
Boring as any yawn
And it still seems to be going on

(1968)

REMEMBERING
VASKO POPA

Vasko Popa in California, 1970

In the fall of 1969, Charles Simic phoned me from the East Coast. He was calling to inform me that Vasko Popa had been invited to an international poetry symposium to be held in Washington, DC, the following spring. The State Department had asked Charlie to be Popa's host on the East Coast, and he— knowing I had dedicated my first book to Popa, and that a long article comparing my poetry and Popa's had been published in the leading literary journal in Yugoslavia—had suggested me as Popa's host on the West Coast. Was I interested?

For the next few months we planned and arranged the tour. After Washington, Popa would have several readings on the East Coast, in the South, and at the new international translation center Paul Engle had set up at the University of Iowa. I would pick Popa up in San Francisco, have him read at Cabrillo College, where I taught, and, through my connections with future Nobel prize-winner Czeslaw Milosz, would provide him with a reading at the University of California at Berkeley, sponsored by the Slavic languages department. Milosz, who had never met Popa, was excited at the prospect of meeting him, and said he would host a party at his house after the reading.

The week before Popa was to arrive on the West Coast, Charlie called with last-minute instructions. The tour had gone well on the East Coast and Popa's appearance at the poetry festival in Washington had been a big success, but Charlie wanted to warn me about two things. The first was not to talk about any politically touchy subject with Popa, since the State Department interpreter, who was accompanying him, seemed to be trying to bait Popa into making anti-Tito comments. Or so Popa thought. And second — and most important — I was to tell Popa I preferred red wine over white and make sure I had a good supply of red wine on hand, preferably pinot noir.

"What's that about?" I asked.

"Vasko's first impressions of a person are all-important," Charlie said, "and he's decided that people who drink red wine exhibit preferences that show them to be people he can trust."

"Anything else?"

"Yes. The State Department is worried about security. They know Watsonville is populated by Croats, and Popa is not only a communist, he's a Serb."

"Not to worry. But I'll keep my eyes open," I replied.

I met Popa at the San Francisco airport on a raw, gray day in early spring. He was a big, shambling man, over six foot four inches tall, with jet black hair and sad black eyes. The pain I thought I detected in those eyes was accentuated by the pronounced bags under them. He was wearing a loose-fitting, extremely lightweight brown suit and no topcoat.

The interpreter introduced us, and Popa, staring into my eyes, gripped both my arms, and greeted me with a short stream of words in Serbo-Croat, searching my face for the answer.

"Mr. Popa ask, do you like white wine or red wine?"

"Tell him red wine," I answered in the same somber tone in which the question had been asked. When Popa heard my answer, he broke into a smile and hugged me to him.

"Good, good," he said.

Popa walked arm-in-arm with me to the baggage area, making faces and rolling his eyes at the interpreter who was walking ahead of us. I nodded that I understood the situation, and he was relieved. Vasko spoke only a few words of English, and was unhappy that I did not speak French, but we overcame the language barrier in ingenious ways in the days to come, and communicated, with difficulty, on the walks in the woods we took without the interpreter's presence.

After I picked up their suitcases, I drove down the coast to Santa Cruz. Popa, the interpreter said, wanted to see the Pacific

Ocean, which was fine with me; I had planned to show him the ocean on the drive south to Santa Cruz anyway.

As we drove down the winding coastline, Popa became more and more excited, expostulating wildly.

"Mr. Popa requests we stop near ocean," the interpreter said.

I had been planning that, too, and when we approached one of my favorite beaches, a tidy expanse of sand surrounded by low, worn-down bluffs, I pulled in. "Tell him this is Bean Hollow Beach, called Frijoles Beach in Spanish." Popa repeated the Spanish aloud after the interpreter explained what I had said. I parked on a small rise over the beach, and we piled out of my Volkswagen.

The weather was still gray and raw. Popa ran ahead of us, his brown suit billowing in the sea wind, sprinting from one patch of wild plant life to another, snatching a handful of succulents here, and scooping up wildflowers there, until he had an armload of flora. Then he marched into the freezing ocean up to his thighs and, casting his bouquet onto the water, proclaimed, said the interpreter, a greeting to the Pacific Ocean on behalf of the Yugoslav people.

We finished our ride with Popa's teeth chattering and the heat in the car on high.

If Popa was flamboyant, he was no clown. He was a highly emotional man who also had the canniness of a showman about him. At times, however, he withdrew into a dark if not painful interior, even in the middle of the parties and gatherings of the many people who wanted to meet him.

We managed to find half a dozen people who spoke French, so we could communicate without the help of the interpreter, who was clearly getting on Popa's nerves. They had traveled throughout the country together, and Popa believed the man was a CIA operative who was constantly baiting him, as Charlie had said, into making anti-Titoist statements.

Popa and the interpreter stayed in separate rooms in a downtown motel. Every morning I picked them up and took them to my house in the mountains after we had breakfast. Popa was most relaxed in the mountains, playing with my eldest daughter, Jana, making faces at my youngest, Valerie, and dancing around with both of them. Once he found a ruby ring on the beach, and later that day at the house he withdrew it with great solmenity from his pocket as if it were a magic amulet, and presented it to Jana, vowing to marry her when she grew up. He was charming, and a natural ladies' man who flattered and fawned over my wife, Wilma. But even then, he often withdrew, it seemed to me, into a place full of ghosts and suffering.

Most of the mornings we worked with the interpreter on the poems Popa would read at Cabrillo and the University of California. He had brought with him Charlie's translations of several sequences—"Games," "Bone to Bone," "The Yawn of Yawns," "The White Pebble," and "The Little Box." I had "Games" and several loose poems translated by a Yugoslav professor I knew when I lived in San Francisco, and I had done my own versions from Ann Pennington's translations that had appeared in a Penguin book of Popa's poems the year before. With all these different versions in front of us, and with the interpreter's help, we made new, composite translations, which we read at both places. The interpreter knew next to nothing about poetry; his translations were accurate, but literal, and didn't take into account the metaphorical richness and implications that abounded in the poems, which I, to my own amazement, intuited in line after line. Popa warmed to the task, and we drew closer and closer over the days. I pointed out to him Pennington's limitations, which were similar to the interpreter's, but Popa was loyal to her, his first and official English translator. In the end, he insisted I show Charlie our versions, which he thought were the best, telling me that Charlie was preparing several of the sequences for publication. When I went over them with Charlie several years later, he liked them a lot, but, alas, by that time his versions had come out in book form. The composite translations did, however, act as an impetus for Charlie and I to work together on other Popa pieces, notably the sequence "Give Me Back My Little Rags."

The afternoons, Popa and I spent in conversation—through his interpreter and French speakers I managed to find at Cabrillo. We talked about Europe, the war, his influence on my poetry, and what we were both working on at present. He spoke of his wife, a mathematics professor in Belgrade, whom he missed more with each passing day. Certainly part of his brooding silences, I felt, had to do with simple homesickness.

I took Popa to various restaurants, introduced him to colleagues, and had him attend classes, where the students looked at him as if he were a strange species of human, or a creature from the zoo, mainly because he spoke no English and, when he spoke, the sound of Serbo-Croatian struck their ears as a jumble of noises they had never heard before. But Popa's warmth and friendly smile won them over. They knew they were in the presence of an international celebrity, and listened intently and courteously to anything he said before the interpreter translated his words.

After each class or gathering of colleagues, we would retire to a restaurant or bar, where Popa would drink copious amounts of red wine and sink into a dreamy silence. I got the impression, after a while, that he was performing when he met people, and after the meetings were over, he would withdraw in exhaustion, his eyes flooding with inner pain.

I don't mean to romanticize Popa's distracted withdrawals, but I wasn't imagining them. Many times he struggled to talk to me, it seemed, on a personal level, but the language barrier was too great. Then again the inner pain I thought I detected in him could have been physical, since he had three ulcers he thought he was controlling by drinking his daily quota of red wine. White wine, he thought, exacerbated his condition. But he said red wine bound the ulcers like a healing potion. Whatever the nature of the pain, I saw him many times gnashing his teeth.

Three days after his arrival, we read at Cabrillo. The interpreter reiterated the State Department's security concerns. I alerted the campus police, but felt the concerns were negligible. Although Santa Cruz's large Slavic population was Croat, and Popa was Serbian, I couldn't imagine there would be a problem. I had reserved the cafeteria in the student union for the reading, and had the tables removed and two hundred chairs arranged in rows. I had sent publicity to all the area newspapers, including the San Jose and San Francisco dailies. I had requests for tapes of the reading from several community radio stations in the Bay Area, but nervously wondered if my preparations would draw a respectable crowd, especially since both Popa and the interpreter had spoken unhappily about the small turnouts at his other readings. Both of them retold a number of times with great bitterness his last outing at Tulane, in New Orleans, where they had arrived with their hosts to find the auditorium dark and locked, and finally read to the host and his wife and the auditorium's janitor.

I needn't have worried. Not only did hundreds of students show up, primed by my colleagues and me, but it seemed all of the Croatian population of Watsonville showed up as well. The two hundred seats were quickly filled and students and townspeople stood packed along the walls and in the doorways to the student cafeteria, where the reading was held.

The evening was an unprecedented success, and Popa was extremely moved. Before the reading, many of the old Croats from Watsonville came up to him, greeting him in Serbo-Croat, telling him where their families were from in the old country and expressing their delight that he was there, many of them extending invitations for him to visit them, which we didn't have time to do in Popa's already full schedule. There were so many greetings and introductions that the reading started half an hour later than was scheduled. But everyone was patient, and a festive, expectant mood spread through the crowd as they looked around, recognizing neighbors or classmates, and enjoying the enormity of the event.

I was not about to let the audience's elation deflate. I read the English versions of Popa's poems, and introduced him and the nature of his poetry, specifying what each poem was about, how it worked, and what to listen for, and giving a dramatic reading of each one. "Bone to Bone" brought wild laughter and applause, after I explained that it was a dialogue between two bones that had been buried for some time, but that each one still maintained the personality of the human to whom it had belonged. I also said it was like a dialogue between Estragon and Vladimir in *Waiting for Godot,* and proceeded to read the poem, after Popa's reading of the original in Serbo-Croat, in two different voices. At the conclusion of the reading, the audience jumped to its feet, giving Popa a wild ovation for five minutes. At first he humbly bowed, but as the applause continued, tears came to his eyes, he put his hand on his heart, and hung his head in appreciation. When the cheering stopped, fifty or sixty of the Croats in the audience formed a reception line, each person, teary-eyed, shaking Popa's hand and saying words of approbation to him in Serbo-Croat.

The evening had been emotionally overwhelming, and we left with ten people in tow for a restaurant I had arranged to remain open for an after-hours snack — and the inevitable red wine. Popa was expansive, but depleted. His arm was continually draped around my shoulders. We had become closer than ever, since the reading had gone better than he had imagined. I had also taken care of every one of his needs during the four previous days. In fact, Popa let it be known through the interpreter that I was taking care of him too well, and he was calling me, with an affectionate smile, "my slave." At the same time, we had learned to nod and wink to communicate without words, especially in light of the interpreter's supposed trouble-making.

The interpreter was certainly smarmy, and his constant smile had struck a false note since the meeting at the airport. He would take me aside or whisper conspiratorially when Popa left the room, hinting at I know not what, and insinuating that we were Americans and Popa was, when all was said and done, a communist, and I should... should what? Nothing was explicitly said, just suggested. The man was irritating, and at an afternoon cocktail party that included my Cabrillo colleagues, he sat back, nodding and smiling, as if he were picking up bits of information he would file in a report to Washington. Maybe I had seen too many spy films, or Popa's paranoia was taking hold of me. But the interpreter's behavior was clearly insinuating and, if nothing else, disturbing.

Ten of us went off to a restaurant after the reading. The group included a French professor from the university, an attractive woman, smartly dressed, with neatly coifed straight brown hair that hugged her head in a short haircut. She and Popa flirted harmlessly, and kept up a running dialogue in French, which she broke off every few moments to explain in English to the rest of us at the table.

The wine continued to appear, served by one of my students, who was the restaurant's night manager, and was keeping the bar open just for us. It was a good restaurant, its wine list excellent, and Popa was enjoying its fine selection of different California pinot noirs, every so often turning to the interpreter, who was muttering to him.

Although he consumed large amounts of wine each day, Popa rarely seemed drunk, but the excitement of the reading and the letdown after it seemed to weaken his constitution, and he was soon inebriated, smiling too broadly. He was also getting more and more annoyed at the interpreter's mutterings, and suddenly he leaped to his feet, reaching into his back pocket, and, taking a card from his wallet, he slapped it on the table, yelling several sentences in Serbo-Croat. The interpreter slunk back in his chair, his face first white, then slowly turning crimson. Still standing, Popa turned to the French professor and said something in French with great vehemence, which she immediately interpreted for us.

"Vasko said he had had enough of this wheedling interpreter and had thrown his Communist party card on the table, telling him to look at it, that he would always be a Communist because the card is signed in blood."

Popa sat down and, in an intense but deliberate voice, explained through the French professor that in the first years of World War II, he had been rounded up with other young Serbs and sent to a concentration camp. Realizing they might well be executed, the entire camp had rushed the wire and escaped, scattering to different parts of Yugoslavia. Popa, as most of the others, went to the mountains and joined Tito, fighting for the partisans until the end of the war.

We sat without speaking at the conclusion of his words, but I thought I had an inkling about at least some of the reasons

Left to right: George Hitchcock, Vasko Popa, the State department interpreter, and Morton Marcus. California, 1970.

for Popa's distracted silences. As for the interpreter, his wheedling ways ended abruptly that evening.

Several days later, after a standing-room-only reading at the University of California and an uproarious party at Milosz's, Popa and the interpreter left for the East Coast. We said warm goodbyes and he kissed me on both cheeks, tears in his eyes, murmuring in broken English, "My little slave." We traded addresses and he commanded me to come to Yugoslavia, where he would have me invited to the annual international poetry festival at Struga.

Over the years we sent notes and good wishes to each other through traveling friends, and finally in 1989 we arranged to meet at his apartment in Belgrade. When I arrived there after spending a week with my second wife's in-laws on the Dalmatian Coast, there was no one home, and downstairs a shopkeeper explained that Popa had broken his leg two weeks before and was convalescing, of all places, on the Dalmatian Coast. Ironically, I had been within ten miles of where he was staying. I was flying from Belgrade to Athens, and there was no backtracking allowed on my airline ticket. On the flight to Athens that night I outlined the following poem, which not only described my attempt to find Popa in Belgrade, but sought to analyze and encapsulate his poetry.

LOOKING FOR VASKO POPA

Nothing could be less appropriate
than to think of Eliot's winding stair
as I grope my way from landing to landing
in this old apartment house in Belgrade.
The stairs are unlit, and for three floors
I follow a shadowy elevator's iron cage,
shuffling through tumble-down plaster,
newspapers, bottles, and cellophane,
sniffing collapsed oranges and sour wine,
cigarette smoke, oiled machinery, and grime
before I arrive at the old poet's door.

He isn't home. I knock again and listen,
imagining him in a room down a dusty hall,
helpless in a chair, his eyes bulging
as he struggles to work his lips.
Listen, there is only the drone of wind
beneath the door, and again I think of Eliot,
his final silence echoing down his last years
as down a stairwell like this one,

where he saw himself as an old man
still gripping the banister at the bottom step.

Downstairs a plump little shopkeeper,
who speaks no English, grips his thigh
and hops to the right, trying to tell me,
with whistles and grunts, that the poet
broke his leg and has been convalescing
hundreds of miles away, at the seaside.
Images of Eliot rise again: the Fisher King
revitalized, with slashes on his thigh—
imprinted impotence in a hop,
a stutter step, that is one of the meanings
the shopkeeper's pantomime ludicrously implies.
The other is the absence here of a poet's
precise use of words to perfectly describe
the all too apparent imperfection of men.

To think of Eliot at a time like this:
nothing could be less fitting than the dry,
deliberate poetics of the English don
in comparison to the poet I search for here,
a maker of ten-page epics, where bones
don' t chirp but comically debate, pliers
with broken jaws, like discarded workmen,
are thrown out of windows, and the combined
sides of triangles, sliding on fiery tracks,
equal human destiny.
                            And yet, and yet—
both poets walked among the multitudes
and looked for meaning after major wars,
the Englishman in old books and rusty symbols,

arriving in the end at the arthritic ceremonies
of a doddering church, while this poet,
whose apartment is approached by stumbling
through the rubbish of an age, found meaning
in his native folklore and the fellowship
of mountain fighters defending their land.
All this he compressed into a pristine music,
chimes of sunlight and wind pinging
over an endless line of refugees—
a raised arm, a hammer flying into the air,
an eye peeking from behind a cart.
He made a mythology of this, his people's history:
populations fleeing for their lives,
slaughtering others or those in their ranks,
or flowing through the landscape
on an endless pilgrimage—human parts
seen for a moment and then gone,
as in a crowd we glimpse a shoulder
or the swagger of someone familiar,
or watch a teapot roll from a thicket of legs,
which hands immediately grab, returning it
to the anonymous mass of moving bodies.

He distilled these elements into cosmic yawns
and magic kettles, added the star charts
glinting in the joints of every skeleton,
and made of them all a secondary heaven.
He never abandoned these images of the lost,
now pliers crushing a nail's head,
now pebbles and triangles scurrying
after their gluttonous, comic-book ends,
until he seemed to live in a huge room,

surrounded by clocks and discarded flywheels,
where broken lips and overturned eyeballs—
once the smiles and frightened eyes of dolls—
littered the floor around his easy chair,
and runaway teeth, galloping in cavalry charges
back and forth across the carpet, dashed
headlong into the walls, scattering like dice
before they re-formed their clattering ranks
in readiness for yet another charge.
All the while, the poet did not dare to move,
afraid he might trample his tiny charges or knock over
the miniature kettles and dancing shoes
on the table near his elbow. Nor could he
call out in a voice that might deafen them,
even to answer the pounding down the hall
where someone was knocking on his apartment door.

    I never did get to meet Popa again. He died two years later
at the age of sixty-eight, just before the break-up of the Yugoslav
federation and the wars in Croatia and Bosnia.

Vasko Popa

Vasko Popa was one of the major poets of the twentieth century. Although he wrote in Serbian, a language spoken by less than twenty-four million people, his poetry garnered praise far and wide for its inventiveness, imagery and vision and was translated into twenty languages. He was hailed as a great poet of his time by Mexican poet and Nobel Prize winner, Octavio Paz, and Ted Hughes, poet laureate of Britain and an early and continuing admirer, in 1968 commented that Popa's "vision was vast and one understands why he has been called an epic poet." In 1978 Hughes observed, "As Popa penetrates deeper into his life, with book after book, it begins to look like a Universe passing through a Universe. It is one of the most exciting things in modern poetry, to watch this journey being made."

Born in 1922, Popa fought as a Yugoslav partisan in World War II and was held in a Nazi concentration camp. After the war he studied at the universities of Vienna, Bucharest and Belgrade, receiving a degree in French and Yugolsav Literature from Belgrade. He spent his life as an editor working in various Yugoslav publishing houses. He died at the age of sixty-eight in 1991, just before the outbreak of the civil wars that shattered the Yugoslav federation.

MORTON MARCUS

Morton Marcus is the author of ten volumes of poetry and one novel, including *The Santa Cruz Mountain Poems, Pages From A Scrapbook of Immigrants, Moments Without Names: New & Selected Prose Poems* and *Shouting Down The Silence: Verse Poems 1988-2001.* In 2007, he published a new volume of prose poems, *Pursuing The Dream Bone,* and last year (2008) his literary memoirs, *Striking Through The Masks,* was published. He has had more than 450 poems published in literary journals, his work has been selected to appear in over ninety anthologies, and he has read his poems and taught creative writing workshops at universities throughout the nation and in Europe.

Marcus taught English and film at Cabrillo College for thirty years before his retirement in 1998. In 1999, he was selected to be Santa Cruz County Artist of the Year, and in 2007 he was a recipient of a Gail Rich Award for his contributions to Santa Cruz culture. For twenty-four years, he has been the co-host of *The Poetry Show,* the longest running poetry radio program in the nation. A film historian and critic as well as poet, his reviews appear regularly in West Coast newspapers, and for the past ten years he has been the co-host of a television film review show called *Cinema Scene,* which broadcasts in the San Francisco Bay area and as a podcast at Cinema Scene.Org. His website is www.mortonmarcus.com.

THE TERRA INCOGNITA SERIES
Writing from Central Europe

Series Editor: Aleš Debeljak

Volume 6
Perched on Nothing's Branch
Poems by Attila Jozsef
Edited by Peter Hargitai
80 PAGES $14.00

Volume 5
The City and the Child
Poems by Aleš Debeljak
96 PAGES $14.00

Volume 4
Afterwards: Slovenian Writing 1945-1995
Edited by Andrew Zawacki
250 PAGES $17.00

Volume 3
Heart of Darkness
Poems by Ferida Duraković
112 PAGES $14.00

Volume 2
The Road to Albasan
An Essay by Edmund Keeley
116 PAGES $14.00

Volume 1
The Four Questions of Melancholy
New and Selected Poems of Tomaž Šalamun
Edited by Christopher Merrill
266 PAGES $15.00